The "*Gadget Book*"
For Travelers

by

J. Ronald Adair

Published by

ELTEK Publishing

V 1.0

Introduction

gadget

(ˈgædʒɪt)

n

1. a small mechanical device or appliance
2. any object that is interesting for its ingenuity or novelty rather than for its practical use

While neither of the above definitions are *exactly* applicable to this book, the overall design of it is definitely novel – and we hope it proves to have practical use also.

Although there are many journals from day planners to coloring books, there seemed to be a need for a journal targeted to a specific group of people. Who are these? They are people on the go, creative, with a desire to take control of their travel records.

The Gadget Book is a way of doing this.

There are several sections; references, driving trips, short trips, extended trips, and accumulative records. Each of the trip sections have multiple 'sets' of panels and pages with the first page being an information page, followed by useful pages that are travel specific. The sets may be used individually or be linked via a page reference for a lengthier record.

Thank you for your purchase and good travels!

This Journal is the Property of

____

____

Section 1 – References

This section contains many useful documents, charts and forms for your travel benefit.

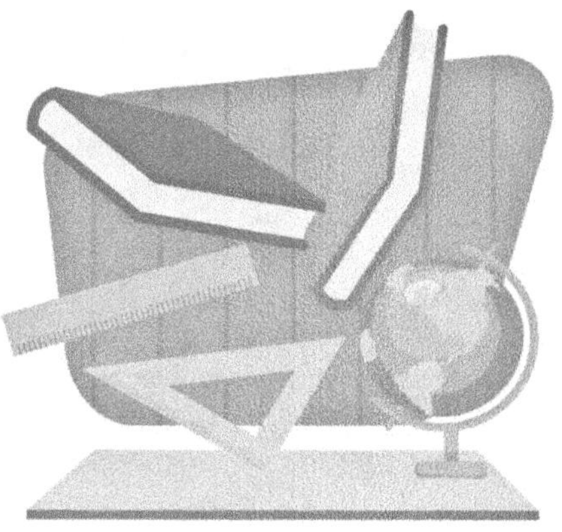

GREENLAND
CANADA
UNITED STATES
MEXICO
BRAZIL
PERU
BOLIVIA
ARGENTINA
RUSSIA
KAZAKHSTAN
UZBEKISTAN
TURKEY
IRAN
AFGHANISTAN
PAKISTAN
CHINA
INDIA
ALGERIA
LIBYA
EGYPT
CHAD
NIGER
ETHIOPIA
D.R. OF THE CONGO
ZAMBIA
NAMIBIA
YEMEN
INDONESIA
AUSTRALIA

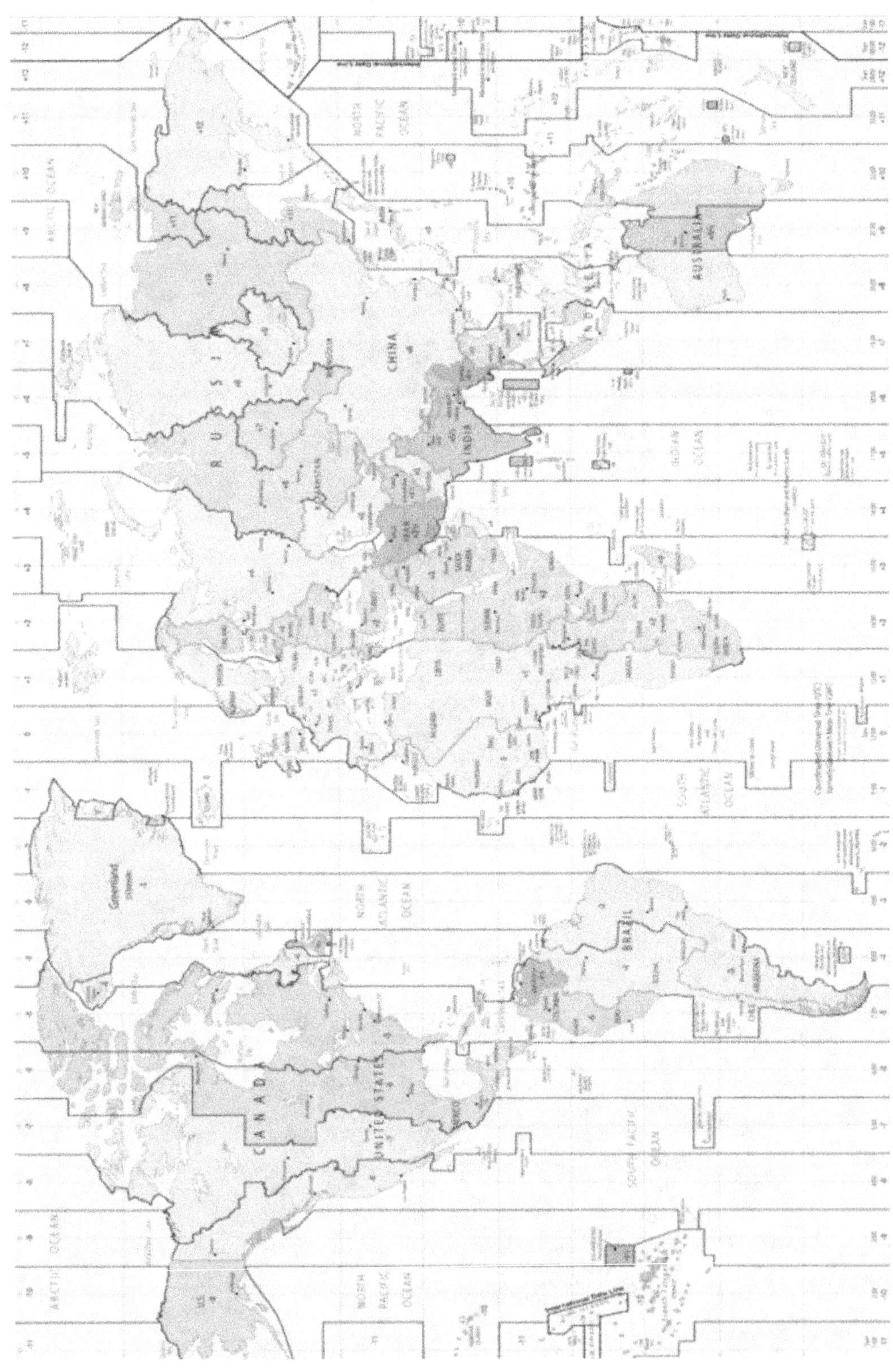

ARCTIC OCEAN
NORTH PACIFIC OCEAN
CHINA
RUSSIA
INDIA
AUSTRALIA
INDIAN OCEAN
Greenland
NORTH ATLANTIC OCEAN
CANADA
UNITED STATES
BRAZIL
SOUTH ATLANTIC OCEAN
SOUTH PACIFIC OCEAN
ARCTIC OCEAN
NORTH PACIFIC OCEAN

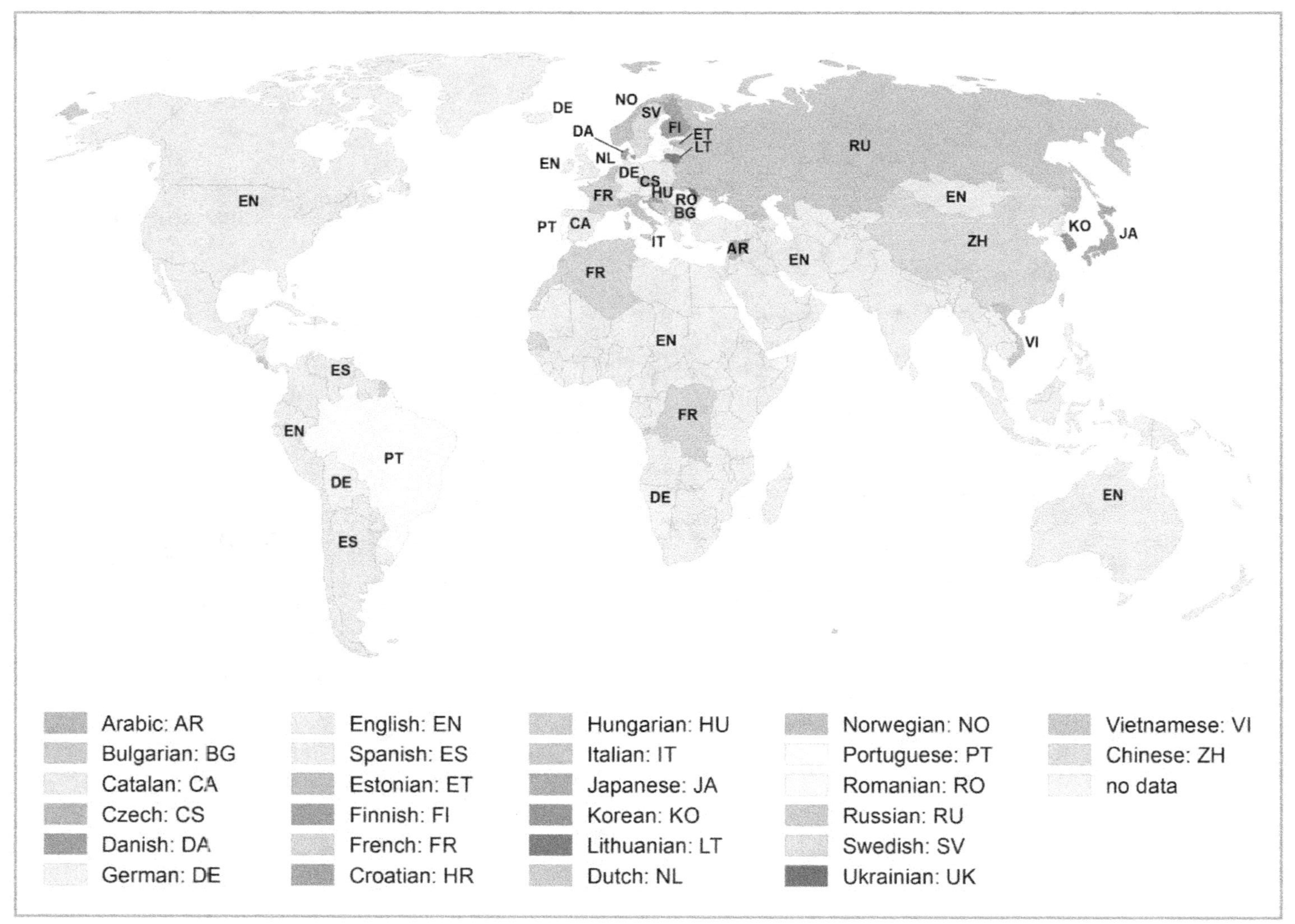

Arabic: AR
Bulgarian: BG
Catalan: CA
Czech: CS
Danish: DA
German: DE
English: EN
Spanish: ES
Estonian: ET
Finnish: FI
French: FR
Croatian: HR
Hungarian: HU
Italian: IT
Japanese: JA
Korean: KO
Lithuanian: LT
Dutch: NL
Norwegian: NO
Portuguese: PT
Romanian: RO
Russian: RU
Swedish: SV
Ukrainian: UK
Vietnamese: VI
Chinese: ZH
no data

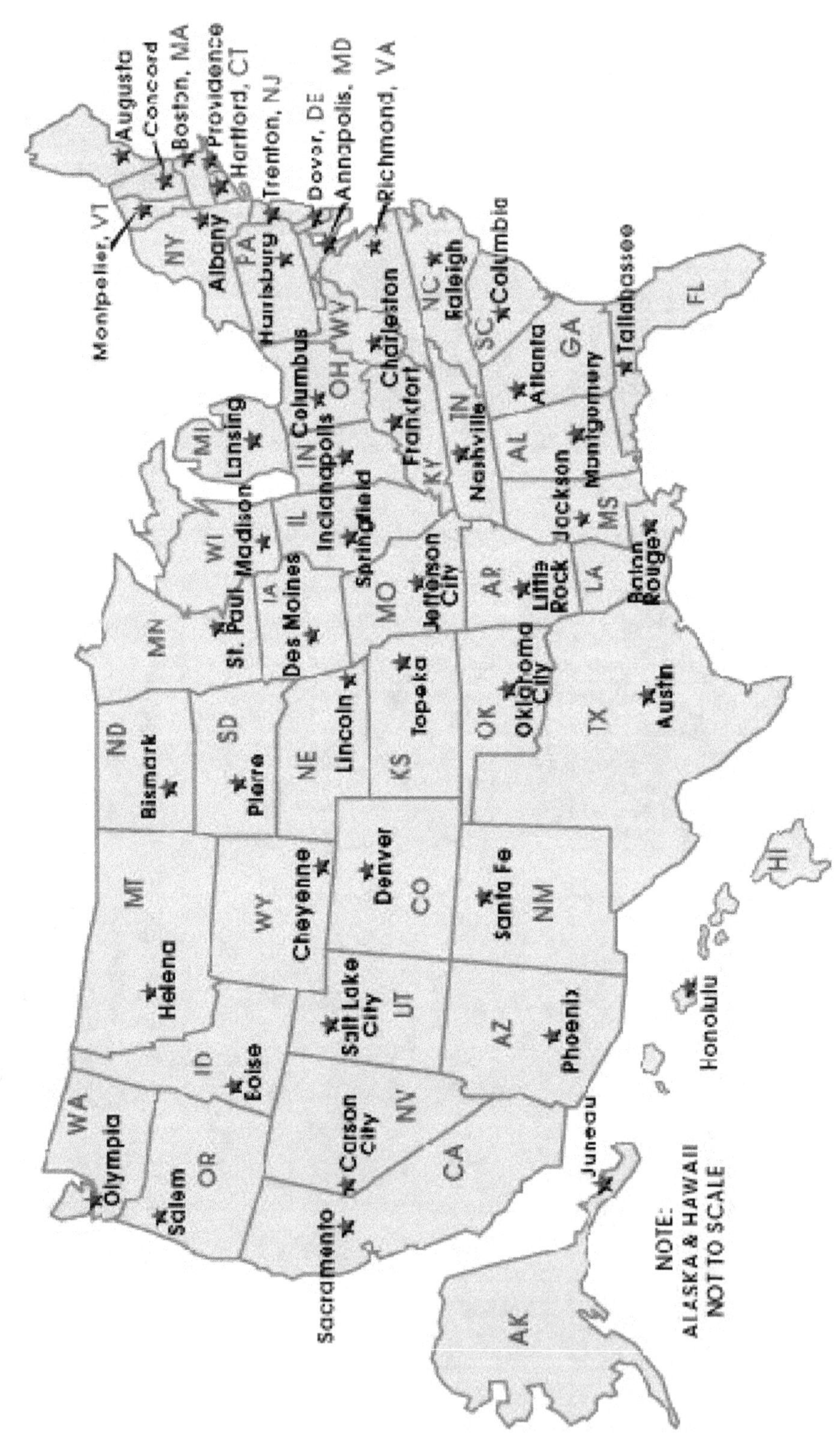
Augusta
Concord
Boston, MA
Providence
Hartford, CT
Trenton, NJ
Dover, DE
Annapolis, MD
Richmond, VA
Montpelier, VT
NY
Albany
PA
Harrisburg
OH
WV
Charleston
NC
Raleigh
SC
Columbia
FL
Tallahassee
MI
Lansing
IN
Columbus
Frankfort
KY
IN
Nashville
GA
Atlanta
AL
Montgomery
WI
Madison
IL
Indianapolis
Springfield
MS
Jackson
LA
Baton Rouge
IA
St. Paul
Des Moines
MN
MO
Jefferson City
AR
Little Rock
ND
Bismark
SD
Pierre
NE
Lincoln
KS
Topeka
OK
Oklahoma City
TX
Austin
MT
Helena
WY
Cheyenne
CO
Denver
NM
Santa Fe
HI
Honolulu
WA
Olympia
ID
Boise
UT
Salt Lake City
AZ
Phoenix
OR
Salem
NV
Carson City
CA
Sacramento
Juneau
AK
NOTE:
ALASKA & HAWAII
NOT TO SCALE

Europe Map

Denmark Strait
Sea
Norwegian Sea
ICELAND
Reykjavík
NORWAY
Kiruna
Tromsø
Murmansk
White Sea
Arkhangel'sk
Luleå
Oulu
FINLAND
SWEDEN
Trondheim
Umeå
Tampere
Gulf of Bothnia
Faroe Islands (DENMARK)
Tórshavn
SHETLAND ISLANDS
Gävle
Turku
Helsinki
St. Petersburg
Rockall (U.K.)
Bergen
Oslo
ORKNEY ISLANDS
HEBRIDES
Stavanger
Göteborg
Stockholm
ÅLAND ISLANDS
Tallinn
ESTONIA
RUSSIA
Moscow
Lake Onega
Gulf of Finland
North Atlantic Ocean
Aberdeen
Gotland
LATVIA
Rīga
Vitsyebsk
Smolensk
North Sea
Glasgow
Edinburgh
DENMARK
Copenhagen
Malmö
Öland
Baltic Sea
LITHUANIA
Vilnius
Mahilyow
Minsk
UNITED
Belfast
Isle of Man (U.K.)
Kaliningrad
Russia
Homyel'
BELARUS
IRELAND
Dublin
Leeds
Manchester
Liverpool
Bornholm
Gdańsk
Hrodna
KINGDOM
Celtic Sea
Cardiff
Birmingham
Hamburg
Bremen
Berlin
Poznań
Warsaw
Brest
Kiev
London
NETH.
Amsterdam
Rotterdam
POLAND
Łódź
English Channel
Essen
Leipzig
Wrocław
L'viv
UKRAINE
Guernsey (U.K.)
Jersey (U.K.)
Brussels
Lille
BEL.
Cologne
Bonn
GERMANY
Frankfurt am Main
Prague
CZECH REPUBLIC
Brno
Kraków
Chernivtsi
Paris
LUX.
Luxembourg
Stuttgart
SLOVAKIA
Bratislava
L'viv
Mykolayiv
Chişinău
Iaşi
MOLDOVA
Odesa
Nantes
Strasbourg
Munich
LIECH.
Vienna
Budapest
Cluj-Napoca
ROMANIA
Zürich
Bern
Vaduz
AUSTRIA
HUNGARY
SWITZ.
Geneva
Ljubljana
FRANCE
Lyon
Milan
Venice
SLOVENIA
Zagreb
Bucharest
Constanţa
Bay of Biscay
Turin
Genoa
CROATIA
BOSNIA AND HERZEGOVINA
Belgrade
Serbia
Black Sea
Varna
Bordeaux
SAN MARINO
Sarajevo
BULGARIA
Bilbao
Toulouse
MONACO
Florence
Montenegro
Sofia
İstanbul
Porto
Andorra la Vella
Marseille
Ligurian Sea
Podgorica
Skopje
F.Y.R.O.M.
Bursa
PORTUGAL
Madrid
ANDORRA
Corsica (FRANCE)
ITALY
Rome
Tiranë
ALB.
Thessaloniki
TURKEY
İzmir
Lisbon
SPAIN
Valencia
Barcelona
Balearic Sea
VATICAN CITY
Naples
GREECE
Athens
Aegean Sea
Sevilla
Sardinia
BALEARIC ISLANDS
Tyrrhenian Sea
Adriatic Sea
Ionian Sea
Rhodes
Gibraltar (U.K.)
Málaga
Algiers
Cagliari
Palermo
Sicily
Crete
Ceuta (SPAIN)
Melilla (SPAIN)
Oran
Tunis
Valletta
MALTA
Scale 1: 19,500,000
Rabat
Casablanca
MOROCCO
ALGERIA
TUNISIA
Mediterranean Sea
0   300 Kilometers
0   300 Miles

Europe Languages

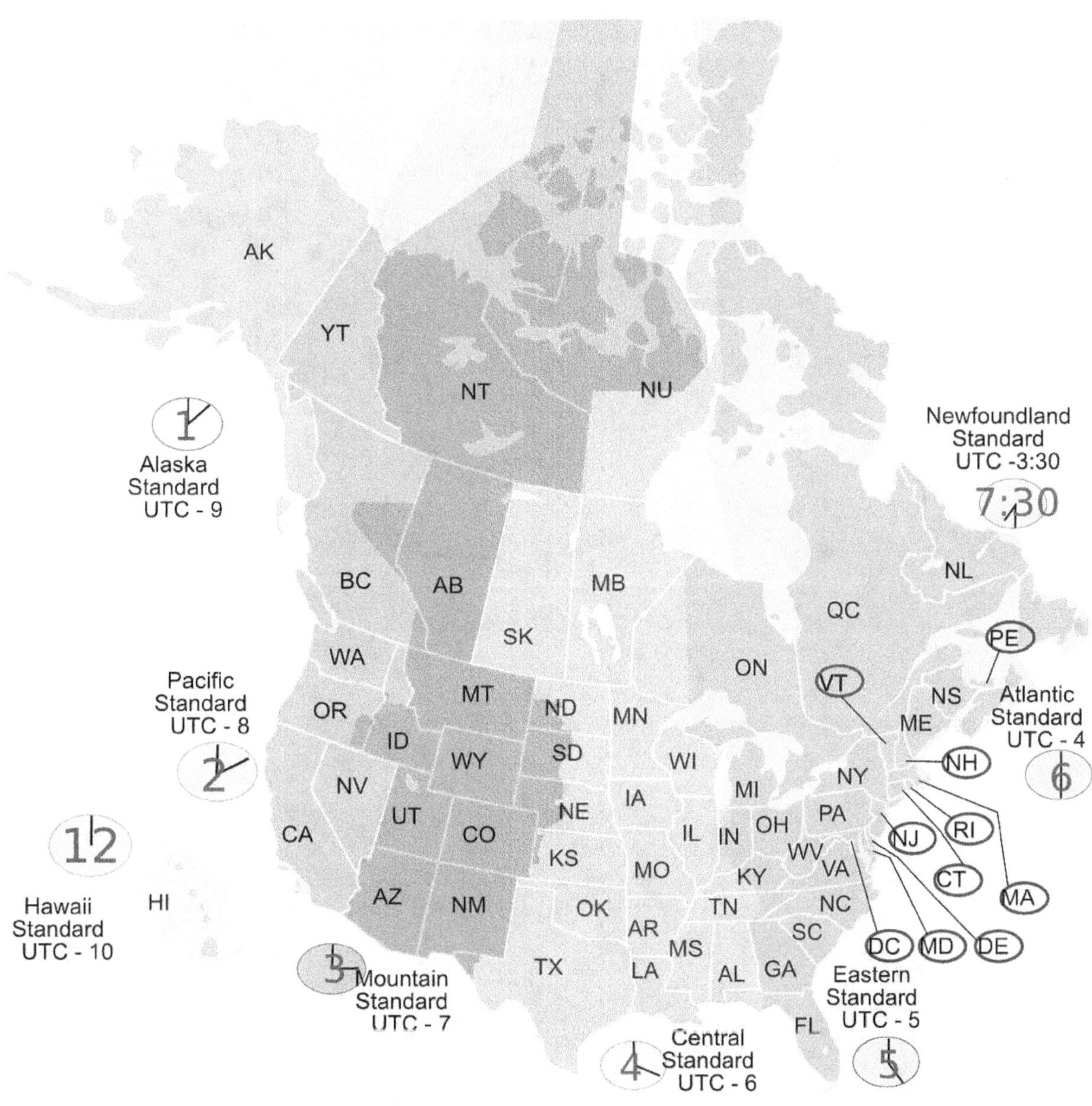

AK
YT
NT
NU
Newfoundland Standard UTC -3:30
7:30
Alaska Standard UTC - 9
BC
AB
SK
MB
QC
NL
PE
Pacific Standard UTC - 8
WA
OR
MT
ID
WY
NV
UT
CA
CO
ND
SD
NE
KS
MN
IA
WI
ON
VT
NS
ME
NH
Atlantic Standard UTC - 4
NY
PA
MI
IL
IN
OH
WV
VA
NJ
RI
CT
MA
12
HI
Hawaii Standard UTC - 10
AZ
NM
OK
MO
KY
TN
NC
SC
DC
MD
DE
Mountain Standard UTC - 7
TX
AR
MS
LA
AL
GA
FL
Eastern Standard UTC - 5
Central Standard UTC - 6

USA Cruise Ports

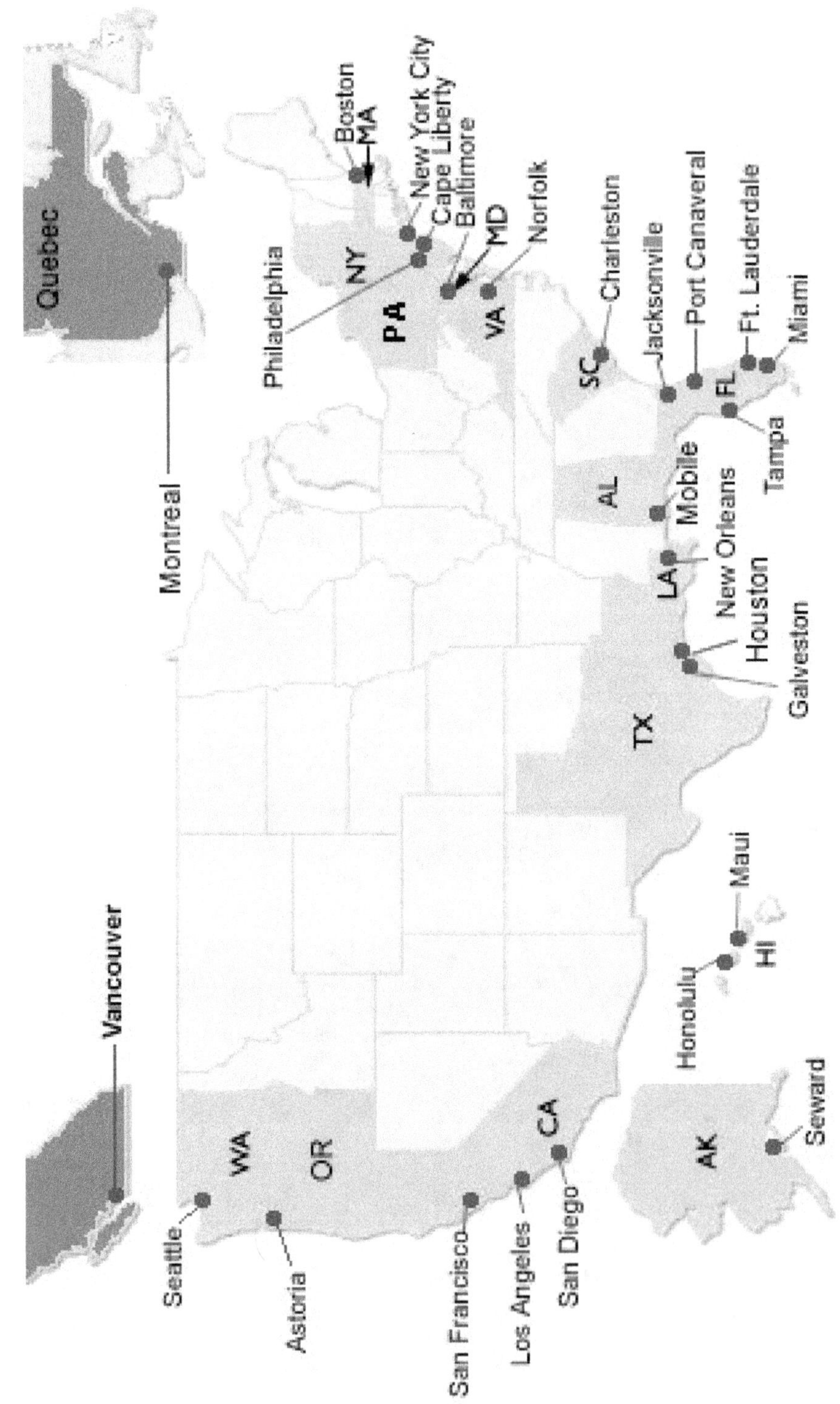

USA Speed Limits by State

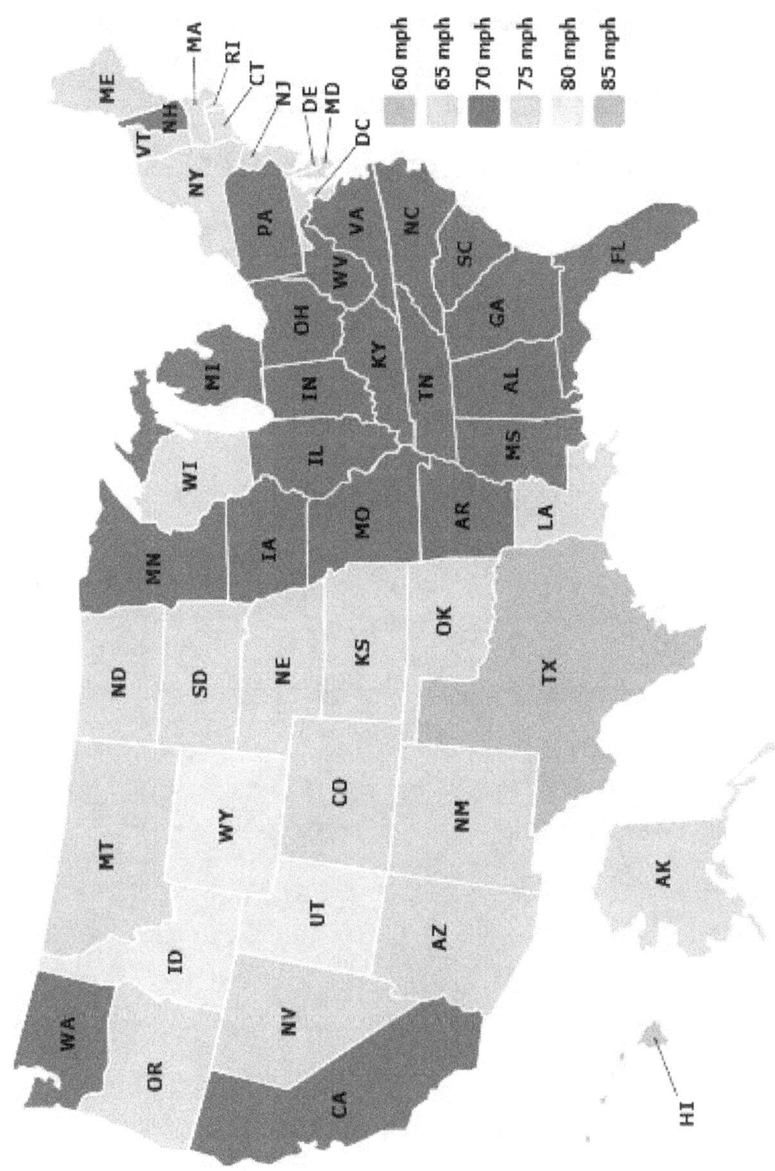

European speed limits

Non-urban roads (excluding autoroutes), selected countries

from 90 to 100 kph   90   80   70

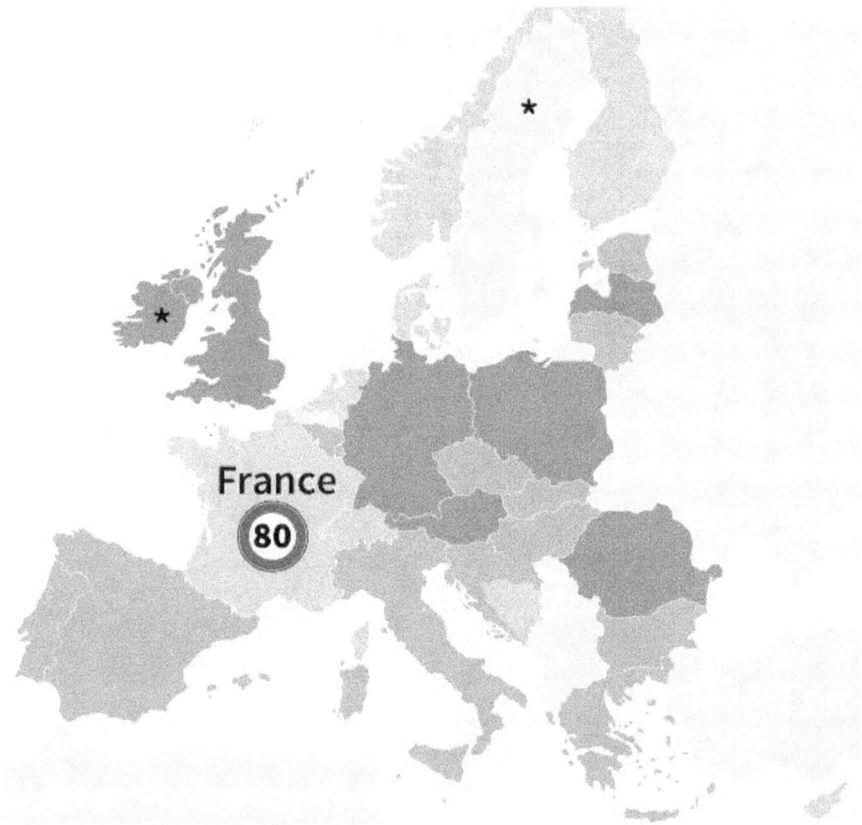

** Ireland: 80 - 100 kph, Sweden: 70 - 80 kph*

Source: European Commission

US Customs Declaration Form (Sample)

U.S. Customs and Border Protection

Customs Declaration

19 CFR 122.27, 148.12, 148.13, 148.110,148.111, 1498; 31 CFR 5316

FORM APPROVED
OMB NO. 1651-0009

Each arriving traveler or responsible family member must provide the following information (only ONE written declaration per family is required). The term "family" is defined as "members of a family residing in the same household who are related by blood, marriage, domestic relationship, or adoption."

1 Family **Name**

First (Given)   Middle

2 **Birth date**   Month   Day   Year

3 Number of **Family members** traveling with you

4 (a) U.S. Street **Address** (hotel name/destination

(b) City   (c) State

5 **Passport issued by** (country)

6 **Passport number**

7 Country of **Residence**

8 **Countries visited** on this trip prior to U.S. arrival

9 **Airline/Flight No.** or **Vessel Name**

10 The primary purpose of this trip is **business:**   Yes   No

11 I am (We are) bringing
(a) fruits, vegetables, plants, seeds, food, insects: Yes   No
(b) meats, animals, animal/wildlife products: Yes   No
(c) disease agents, cell cultures, snails: Yes   No
(d) soil or have been on a farm/ranch/pasture: Yes   No

12 I have (We have) been in close proximity of **livestock:**   Yes   No
(such as touching or handling)

13 I am (We are) carrying **currency or monetary instruments** over $10,000 U.S. or foreign equivalent: Yes   No
(see definition of monetary instruments on reverse)

14 I have (We have) **commercial merchandise:**   Yes   No
(articles for sale, samples used for soliciting orders, or goods that are not considered personal effects)

15 **RESIDENTS**—the total value of all goods, including commercial merchandise I/we have purchased or acquired abroad, (including gifts for someone else, but not items mailed to the U.S.) and am/are bringing to the U.S. is: $

VISITORS—the total value of all articles that will remain in the U.S., including commercial merchandise is: $

Read the instructions on the back of this form. Space is provided to list all the items you must declare.

I HAVE READ THE IMPORTANT INFORMATION ON THE REVERSE SIDE OF THIS FORM AND HAVE MADE A TRUTHFUL DECLARATION.

X ___________________

Signature   Date (month/day/year)   CBP Form 6059B (04/14)

AIR POCKET - a transient jolt of turbulence.

ALL-CALL - a request that each flight attendant report via intercom from his or her station.

ALLEY - a taxiway or passageway between terminals or RAMPS.

APRON - Basically any expanse of TARMAC that is not a runway or taxiway — i.e. areas where planes park or are otherwise serviced.

AREA OF WEATHER - This typically means thunderstorms or a zone of heavy precipitation.

ATC – Air Traffic Control.

DEPLANE - the opposite of boarding an aircraft.

DEADHEAD – refers to a pilot or flight attendant repositioning as part of an on-duty assignment

DIRECT FLIGHT - technically, a direct flight is a routing along which the *flight number* does not change; it has nothing to do with whether the plane stops. However, in practice it is when a flight does not stop from the beginning to the end of a flight.

DOORS TO ARRIVAL AND CROSSCHECK – refers to disarming the doors and emergency slides - crosscheck is a generic term used by pilots and flight attendants that have verified the tasks of others.

EFC TIME - expect further clearance (EFC) time, sometimes called a release time, is the point at which a crew expects to be set free from a HOLDING PATTERN or exempted from a GROUND STOP.

EQUIPMENT – the airplane itself.

FINAL APPROACH - approach when it has reached the last, straight-in segment of the landing pattern — that is, aligned with the extended centerline of the runway, requiring no additional turns or maneuvering.

FINAL AND IMMEDIATE BOARDING CALL - provides more urgency than just "final call" or "last call."

FIRST OFFICER - second in command on the FLIGHT DECK.

FLIGHT DECK – the cockpit.

FLIGHT LEVEL – cruising altitude.

FULL, UPRIGHT AND LOCKED POSITION – Referring to seat position and seat trays.

GROUND STOP - the point when departures to one or more destination are curtailed by ATC, usually due to a traffic backlog.

GATEHOUSE - the gate area or boarding lounge.

HOLDING PATTERN - a racetrack-shaped course flown during weather or traffic delays.

IN RANGE - a common GATEHOUSE announcement during delays, when the plane you're waiting to board hasn't yet landed.

LAST MINUTE PAPERWORK - Everything is buttoned up and the flight is ready for pushback. Last minute paperwork usually refers to the weight-and-balance record, a revision to the flight plan, or waiting for maintenance to deal with a write-up and get the logbook in order.

NONSTOP – this is a flight that has no connection (see Direct Flight).

PRE-BOARD – boarding is open to passengers requiring special assistance.

RAMP - refers to the aircraft and ground vehicle movement areas closest to the terminal — the aircraft parking zones and surrounds.

TARMAC – somewhat synonymous with RAMP.

TAMPERING WITH, DISABLING, OR DESTROYING – tampering with airplane equipment.

THE OFF POSITION – Off.

WHEELS-UP TIME - Refers to the time when a plane is expected to be fully airborne.

AFT - at, near, or toward the stern of a ship (farthest back).

ANCHOR - a heavy object, usually a shaped iron weight with flukes, lowered by cable or chain to the bottom of a body of water to keep a vessel from drifting.

ATRIUM - the central court (or center area) of a cruise ship, usually rising through more than one story or all the stories and having a skylight or glass on one side and/or the roof.

BERTH - a built-in bed or bunk, as in a ship's cabin.

BOAT - a small, open water vehicle propelled by oars, sails, engine, etc.

BOW - the very front of the ship.

BREECHES BUOY - a device for rescuing people at sea, consisting of a piece of strong canvas with leg holes suspended from a life preserver that is run along a rope from ship to shore or to another ship.

BRIDGE - the ship's navigational control center.

BULKHEAD - any of the upright partitions separating parts of a ship as for protection against fire or leakage.

CABIN - a private room on a ship, as a bedroom or office. The terms Cabin and Stateroom are used interchangeably.

CABIN STEWARD - a person whose work is to serve and run errands for the passengers aboard a ship.

CAPTAIN - the person in command of a ship.

DISEMBARK – to unload (passengers or goods) from a ship, aircraft, etc.

DOCK - a large structure or excavated basin for receiving ships, may be equipped with gates to keep water in or out.

DOUBLE OCCUPANCY - refers to a cabin shared by two people.

EMBARK – to go aboard a ship, aircraft, etc.

FLUKE - a pointed part of an anchor, designed to catch in the ground.

FORWARD - toward the front or a point in toward the bow of a ship.

GANGWAY - a passageway for entering (embarking) or leaving (disembarking) from a ship.

LEEWARD - on the side of the ship away from the wind. (As opposed to Windward).

LIFE BOAT - one of the small boats carried by a ship for use if the ship must be abandoned.

LIFE BUOY - a life preserver in the shape of a ring.

LIFE PRESERVER - a buoyant device for saving a person from drowning by keeping the body afloat, as a ring or sleeveless jacket of canvas-covered cork.

LIFE VEST OR JACKET - a life preserver in the form of a sleeveless jacket or vest.

MUSTER – to come together or gather - for instance, for inspection or roll call.

MUSTER STATION – a specific location on the ship to gather, based on cabin assignment.

NAUTICAL - of or having to do with sailors, ships, or navigation. A unit of speed of one nautical mile (6,076.12 feet or 1,852 meters) an hour: abbrev. kn or kt [to average a speed of 10 knots]

PIER – a structure built out over the water and supported by pillars or piles: used as a landing place.

PORT - the left-hand side of a ship or boat as one faces forward as opposed to starboard.

PORT OF CALL - regular stopover(s) on a cruise itinerary.

PURSER - a ship's officer in charge of accounts, freight, tickets, etc., esp. on a passenger vessel.

QUAD CABIN – a cabin that accommodates four passengers.

SHIP – any water vehicle of considerable size navigating deep water, especially one powered by an engine.

STARBOARD – the right-hand side of a ship or boat as one faces forward as opposed to Port.

STATEROOM - a private cabin on a ship.

STERN - the rear end of a ship or boat.

TENDER - a boat for carrying passengers to or from a ship close to shore.

VESSEL - any relatively large watercraft.

WINDWARD - on the side of the ship from which the wind blows; toward the wind. (As opposed to Leeward)

U.S. Department of Transportation https://www.transportation.gov/

Bureau of Transportation Statistics https://www.bts.gov/rita

International Travel – Health Issues https://travel.state.gov/content/travel/en/international-travel/before-you-go/your-health-abroad/insurance-providers-overseas.html

https://travel.state.gov/content/travel/en/international-travel/before-you-go/your-health-abroad.html

USA FHWA Rout Finder List https://www.fhwa.dot.gov/planning/national_highway_system/interstate_highway_system/routefinder/index.cfm

Air Flights Tracker https://www.flightview.com/

Cruise Ships Tracker https://www.cruisemapper.com/ , https://www.livecruiseshiptracker.com/,

USA Driving Weather Forecast http://www.intellicast.com/Travel/Driving/Highways.aspx

Travelers Aid International https://www.travelersaid.org/

Adventure Road (USA Road Trips) https://www.adventureroad.com/

World Travel (Lonely Planet) https://www.lonelyplanet.com/

Europe Travel https://visiteurope.com/en/

TSA (USA) https://www.tsa.gov/

Federal Aviation Assoc. (USA) https://www.faa.gov/travelers/

USDA Pet Travel Policies https://www.aphis.usda.gov/aphis/pet-travel

Passports and International Travel https://www.usa.gov/travel-abroad

Country Checklist https://travel.state.gov/content/travel/en/international-travel/International-Travel-Country-Information-Pages.html

Section 2 – Driving Trips

This section is designed for driving trips, either by automobile or bus and usually up to 7 days in length. For extended road trips, you may link several of these entries together with the 'Link to page' feature.

Trip Preparation Checklist

Trip:	Start Date:	End Date:
Destination:		Trip Length:
Purpose:	Travel Mode:	
Departure Point:	Arrival Point:	

Stopovers:

Documents req'd:

Tickets (if req'd):

Travel party Names:

Clothing/Personal Items:

Medicines/Medical:

Games/Electronics to take:

Language/translation aids:

Pet(s) arrangements:

Mail/Package pick-up:

Landscape maintenance arrangement:

Home security arrangement:

Food/snacks to take:

Bill payment arrangements:

Auto Preparation:

Other items not covered:

Link to Page __________

Trip Itinerary

Places to Go:	Notes:

Things to See:	Notes:

Trip Conclusion

Places of Interest

Date	Location	Category

People Met or Contacts Made

Date	Name	Addr/Number

Trip Expense Record

Date	Description	Amount

Trip Preparation Checklist

Trip:	Start Date:	End Date:
Destination:		Trip Length:
Purpose:	Travel Mode:	
Departure Point:	Arrival Point:	

Stopovers:

Documents req'd:

Tickets (if req'd):

Travel party Names:

Clothing/Personal Items: _______________ _______________
_______________ _______________ _______________
_______________ _______________ _______________

Medicines/Medical: _______________ _______________
_______________ _______________ _______________

Games/Electronics to take: _______________ _______________
_______________ _______________ _______________

Language/translation aids:

Pet(s) arrangements:

Mail/Package pick-up:

Landscape maintenance arrangement:

Home security arrangement:

Food/snacks to take:

Bill payment arrangements:

Auto Preparation:

Other items not covered:

Link to Page _________

Trip Itinerary

Places to Go:	Notes:

Things to See:	Notes:

Trip Conclusion

Places of Interest		
Date	Location	Category

People Met or Contacts Made		
Date	Name	Addr/Number

Trip Expense Record		
Date	Description	Amount

Trip Preparation Checklist

Trip:		Start Date:	End Date:
Destination:			Trip Length:
Purpose:		Travel Mode:	
Departure Point:		Arrival Point:	

Stopovers:

Documents req'd:

Tickets (if req'd):

Travel party Names:

Clothing/Personal Items:

Medicines/Medical:

Games/Electronics to take:

Language/translation aids:

Pet(s) arrangements:

Mail/Package pick-up:

Landscape maintenance arrangement:

Home security arrangement:

Food/snacks to take:

Bill payment arrangements:

Auto Preparation:

Other items not covered:

Link to Page _________

Trip Itinerary

Places to Go:	Notes:

Things to See:	Notes:

Trip Conclusion

Places of Interest

Date	Location	Category

People Met or Contacts Made

Date	Name	Addr/Number

Trip Expense Record

Date	Description	Amount

Trip Preparation Checklist

Trip:		Start Date:	End Date:
Destination:			Trip Length:
Purpose:		Travel Mode:	
Departure Point:		Arrival Point:	

Stopovers:

Documents req'd:

Tickets (if req'd):

Travel party Names:

Clothing/Personal Items: ___________ ___________ ___________

___________ ___________ ___________

___________ ___________ ___________

Medicines/Medical: ___________ ___________

___________ ___________

Games/Electronics to take: ___________ ___________

___________ ___________ ___________

Language/translation aids:

Pet(s) arrangements:

Mail/Package pick-up:

Landscape maintenance arrangement:

Home security arrangement:

Food/snacks to take:

Bill payment arrangements:

Auto Preparation:

Other items not covered:

Link to Page __________

Trip Itinerary

Places to Go:	Notes:

Things to See:	Notes:

Trip Conclusion

Places of Interest

Date	Location	Category

People Met or Contacts Made

Date	Name	Addr/Number

Trip Expense Record

Date	Description	Amount

Trip Preparation Checklist

Trip:	Start Date:	End Date:
Destination:		Trip Length:
Purpose:	Travel Mode:	
Departure Point:	Arrival Point:	

Stopovers:

Documents req'd:

Tickets (if req'd):

Travel party Names:

Clothing/Personal Items:

_____________   _____________   _____________

_____________   _____________   _____________

_____________   _____________   _____________

Medicines/Medical:

_____________   _____________   _____________

_____________   _____________   _____________

Games/Electronics to take:

_____________   _____________   _____________

_____________   _____________   _____________

Language/translation aids:

Pet(s) arrangements:

Mail/Package pick-up:

Landscape maintenance arrangement:

Home security arrangement:

Food/snacks to take:

Bill payment arrangements:

Auto Preparation:

Other items not covered:

Link to Page _________

Trip Itinerary

Places to Go:	Notes:

Things to See:	Notes:

Trip Conclusion

Places of Interest

Date	Location	Category

People Met or Contacts Made

Date	Name	Addr/Number

Trip Expense Record

Date	Description	Amount

Trip Preparation Checklist

Trip:		Start Date:	End Date:
Destination:			Trip Length:
Purpose:		Travel Mode:	
Departure Point:		Arrival Point:	

Stopovers:

Documents req'd:

Tickets (if req'd):

Travel party Names:

Clothing/Personal Items:

Medicines/Medical:

Games/Electronics to take:

Language/translation aids:

Pet(s) arrangements:

Mail/Package pick-up:

Landscape maintenance arrangement:

Home security arrangement:

Food/snacks to take:

Bill payment arrangements:

Auto Preparation:

Other items not covered:

Link to Page __________

Trip Itinerary

Places to Go:	Notes:

Things to See:	Notes:

Trip Conclusion

Places of Interest		
Date	Location	Category

People Met or Contacts Made		
Date	Name	Addr/Number

Trip Expense Record		
Date	Description	Amount

Trip Preparation Checklist

Trip:	Start Date:	End Date:
Destination:		Trip Length:
Purpose:	Travel Mode:	
Departure Point:	Arrival Point:	
Stopovers:		

Documents req'd:

Tickets (if req'd):

Travel party Names:

Clothing/Personal Items:

Medicines/Medical:

Games/Electronics to take:

Language/translation aids:

Pet(s) arrangements:

Mail/Package pick-up:

Landscape maintenance arrangement:

Home security arrangement:

Food/snacks to take:

Bill payment arrangements:

Auto Preparation:

Other items not covered:

Link to Page __________

Trip Itinerary

Places to Go:	Notes:

Things to See:	Notes:

Trip Conclusion

Places of Interest		
Date	Location	Category

People Met or Contacts Made		
Date	Name	Addr/Number

Trip Expense Record		
Date	Description	Amount

Trip Preparation Checklist

Trip:	Start Date:	End Date:
Destination:		Trip Length:
Purpose:	Travel Mode:	
Departure Point:	Arrival Point:	

Stopovers:

Documents req'd:
Tickets (if req'd):
Travel party Names:

Clothing/Personal Items:	_____________	_____________
_____________	_____________	_____________
_____________	_____________	_____________

Medicines/Medical:	_____________	_____________
_____________	_____________	_____________

Games/Electronics to take:	_____________	_____________
_____________	_____________	_____________

Language/translation aids:
Pet(s) arrangements:
Mail/Package pick-up:
Landscape maintenance arrangement:
Home security arrangement:
Food/snacks to take:
Bill payment arrangements:
Auto Preparation:
Other items not covered:

Link to Page __________

Trip Itinerary

Places to Go:	Notes:

Things to See:	Notes:

Trip Conclusion

Places of Interest		
Date	Location	Category

People Met or Contacts Made		
Date	Name	Addr/Number

Trip Expense Record		
Date	Description	Amount

Trip Preparation Checklist

Trip:		Start Date:	End Date:
Destination:			Trip Length:
Purpose:		Travel Mode:	
Departure Point:		Arrival Point:	
Stopovers:			
Documents req'd:			
Tickets (if req'd):			
Travel party Names:			
Clothing/Personal Items:			
Medicines/Medical:			
Games/Electronics to take:			
Language/translation aids:			
Pet(s) arrangements:			
Mail/Package pick-up:			
Landscape maintenance arrangement:			
Home security arrangement:			
Food/snacks to take:			
Bill payment arrangements:			
Auto Preparation:			
Other items not covered:			

Link to Page __________

Trip Itinerary

Places to Go:	Notes:

Things to See:	Notes:

Trip Conclusion

Places of Interest

Date	Location	Category

People Met or Contacts Made

Date	Name	Addr/Number

Trip Expense Record

Date	Description	Amount

Trip Preparation Checklist

Trip:	Start Date:	End Date:
Destination:		Trip Length:
Purpose:	Travel Mode:	
Departure Point:	Arrival Point:	

Stopovers:

Documents req'd:

Tickets (if req'd):

Travel party Names:

Clothing/Personal Items: ___________ ___________ ___________

___________ ___________ ___________

___________ ___________ ___________

Medicines/Medical: ___________ ___________ ___________

___________ ___________ ___________

Games/Electronics to take: ___________ ___________

___________ ___________

Language/translation aids:

Pet(s) arrangements:

Mail/Package pick-up:

Landscape maintenance arrangement:

Home security arrangement:

Food/snacks to take:

Bill payment arrangements:

Auto Preparation:

Other items not covered:

Link to Page __________

Trip Itinerary

Places to Go:	Notes:

Things to See:	Notes:

Trip Conclusion

Places of Interest		
Date	Location	Category

People Met or Contacts Made		
Date	Name	Addr/Number

Trip Expense Record		
Date	Description	Amount

Section 3 – Short Air/Sea Trips

This section is designed for short trips, usually up to 7 days in length. This could be a driving road trip, a long weekend outing or a short cruise.

No flying machine will ever fly from New York to Paris ... [because] no known motor can run at the requisite speed for four days without stopping.

Orville Wright

Trip Preparation Checklist

| Trip: | Start Date: | End Date: |
| Destination: | | Trip Length: |

Trip:		Start Date:	End Date:
Destination:			Trip Length:
Purpose:		Travel Mode:	
Departure Point:		Arrival Point:	
Stopovers/Connections:			
Documents req'd:			
Carrier (1):	(2):	(3):	
Terminal/Gate Numbers:			
Tickets (if req'd):			
Travel party Names:			
Shuttle/Taxi arrangements:			
Clothing/Personal Items:			
Medicines/Medical:			
Electronics to take:			
Language/translation aids:			
Travel Insurance:			
Pet(s) arrangements:			
Mail/Package pick-up:			
Landscape maintenance arrangement:			
Home security arrangement:			
Food/snacks:			
Bill payment arrangements:			
Other items not covered:			

Link to Page __________

Trip Itinerary

Places to Go:	Notes:

Things to See:	Notes:

Trip Conclusion

Places of Interest		
Date	Location	Category

People Met or Contacts Made		
Date	Name	Addr/Number

Trip Expense Record		
Date	Description	Amount

Trip Preparation Checklist

Trip:	Start Date:	End Date:
Destination:		Trip Length:
Purpose:	Travel Mode:	
Departure Point:	Arrival Point:	

Stopovers/Connections:

Documents req'd:

Carrier (1):	(2):	(3):

Terminal/Gate Numbers:

Tickets (if req'd):

Travel party Names:

Shuttle/Taxi arrangements:

Clothing/Personal Items:

Medicines/Medical:

Electronics to take:

Language/translation aids:

Travel Insurance:

Pet(s) arrangements:

Mail/Package pick-up:

Landscape maintenance arrangement:

Home security arrangement:

Food/snacks:

Bill payment arrangements:

Other items not covered:

Link to Page __________

Trip Itinerary

Places to Go:	Notes:

Things to See:	Notes:

Trip Conclusion

Places of Interest		
Date	Location	Category

People Met or Contacts Made		
Date	Name	Addr/Number

Trip Expense Record		
Date	Description	Amount

Trip Preparation Checklist

Trip:	Start Date:	End Date:
Destination:		Trip Length:
Purpose:	Travel Mode:	
Departure Point:	Arrival Point:	
Stopovers/Connections:		
Documents req'd:		
Carrier (1):	(2):	(3):
Terminal/Gate Numbers:		
Tickets (if req'd):		
Travel party Names:		
Shuttle/Taxi arrangements:		
Clothing/Personal Items:		
Medicines/Medical:		
Electronics to take:		
Language/translation aids:		
Travel Insurance:		
Pet(s) arrangements:		
Mail/Package pick-up:		
Landscape maintenance arrangement:		
Home security arrangement:		
Food/snacks:		
Bill payment arrangements:		
Other items not covered:		

Link to Page __________

Trip Itinerary

Places to Go:	Notes:

Things to See:	Notes:

Trip Conclusion

Places of Interest

Date	Location	Category

People Met or Contacts Made

Date	Name	Addr/Number

Trip Expense Record		
Date	Description	Amount

Trip Preparation Checklist

Trip:		Start Date:	End Date:
Destination:			Trip Length:
Purpose:		Travel Mode:	
Departure Point:		Arrival Point:	
Stopovers/Connections:			
Documents req'd:			
Carrier (1):	(2):	(3):	
Terminal/Gate Numbers:			
Tickets (if req'd):			

Travel party Names:

Shuttle/Taxi arrangements:

Clothing/Personal Items:

Medicines/Medical:

Electronics to take:

Language/translation aids:

Travel Insurance:

Pet(s) arrangements:

Mail/Package pick-up:

Landscape maintenance arrangement:

Home security arrangement:

Food/snacks:

Bill payment arrangements:

Other items not covered:

Link to Page __________

Trip Itinerary

Places to Go:	Notes:

Things to See:	Notes:

Trip Conclusion

Places of Interest		
Date	Location	Category

People Met or Contacts Made		
Date	Name	Addr/Number

Trip Expense Record		
Date	**Description**	**Amount**

Trip Preparation Checklist

Trip:		Start Date:	End Date:
Destination:			Trip Length:
Purpose:		Travel Mode:	
Departure Point:		Arrival Point:	
Stopovers/Connections:			
Documents req'd:			
Carrier (1):	(2):	(3):	
Terminal/Gate Numbers:			
Tickets (if req'd):			
Travel party Names:			
Shuttle/Taxi arrangements:			
Clothing/Personal Items:			
Medicines/Medical:			
Electronics to take:			
Language/translation aids:			
Travel Insurance:			
Pet(s) arrangements:			
Mail/Package pick-up:			
Landscape maintenance arrangement:			
Home security arrangement:			
Food/snacks:			
Bill payment arrangements:			
Other items not covered:			

Link to Page __________

Trip Itinerary

Places to Go:	Notes:

Things to See:	Notes:

Trip Conclusion

Places of Interest		
Date	Location	Category

People Met or Contacts Made		
Date	Name	Addr/Number

Trip Expense Record		
Date	**Description**	**Amount**

Trip Preparation Checklist

Trip:	Start Date:	End Date:
Destination:		Trip Length:
Purpose:	Travel Mode:	
Departure Point:	Arrival Point:	
Stopovers/Connections:		
Documents req'd:		
Carrier (1):	(2):	(3):
Terminal/Gate Numbers:		
Tickets (if req'd):		
Travel party Names:		
Shuttle/Taxi arrangements:		
Clothing/Personal Items:		
Medicines/Medical:		
Electronics to take:		
Language/translation aids:		
Travel Insurance:		
Pet(s) arrangements:		
Mail/Package pick-up:		
Landscape maintenance arrangement:		
Home security arrangement:		
Food/snacks:		
Bill payment arrangements:		
Other items not covered:		

Link to Page __________

Trip Itinerary

Places to Go:	Notes:

Things to See:	Notes:

Trip Conclusion

Places of Interest		
Date	Location	Category

People Met or Contacts Made		
Date	Name	Addr/Number

Trip Expense Record		
Date	Description	Amount

Trip Preparation Checklist

Trip:		Start Date:	End Date:
Destination:			Trip Length:
Purpose:		Travel Mode:	
Departure Point:		Arrival Point:	
Stopovers/Connections:			
Documents req'd:			
Carrier (1):	(2):	(3):	
Terminal/Gate Numbers:			
Tickets (if req'd):			
Travel party Names:			
Shuttle/Taxi arrangements:			
Clothing/Personal Items:			
Medicines/Medical:			
Electronics to take:			
Language/translation aids:			
Travel Insurance:			
Pet(s) arrangements:			
Mail/Package pick-up:			
Landscape maintenance arrangement:			
Home security arrangement:			
Food/snacks:			
Bill payment arrangements:			
Other items not covered:			

Link to Page __________

Trip Itinerary

Places to Go:	Notes:

Things to See:	Notes:

Trip Conclusion

Places of Interest

Date	Location	Category

People Met or Contacts Made

Date	Name	Addr/Number

Trip Expense Record		
Date	**Description**	**Amount**

Trip Preparation Checklist

Trip:	Start Date:	End Date:
Destination:		Trip Length:
Purpose:	Travel Mode:	
Departure Point:	Arrival Point:	
Stopovers/Connections:		
Documents req'd:		
Carrier (1):	(2):	(3):
Terminal/Gate Numbers:		
Tickets (if req'd):		
Travel party Names:		
Shuttle/Taxi arrangements:		
Clothing/Personal Items:		
Medicines/Medical:		
Electronics to take:		
Language/translation aids:		
Travel Insurance:		
Pet(s) arrangements:		
Mail/Package pick-up:		
Landscape maintenance arrangement:		
Home security arrangement:		
Food/snacks:		
Bill payment arrangements:		
Other items not covered:		

Link to Page __________

Trip Itinerary

Places to Go:	Notes:

Things to See:	Notes:

Trip Conclusion

Places of Interest		
Date	Location	Category

People Met or Contacts Made		
Date	Name	Addr/Number

Trip Expense Record		
Date	**Description**	**Amount**

Section 4 – Extended Trips

This section is designed for more extended trips, typically over 7 days in length. This could be a cruise, or 2 week European tour, even a month-long sabatical.

"A vacation is what you take when you can no longer take what you've been taking."
Earl Wilson

Trip Preparation Checklist

Trip:		Start Date:	End Date:
Destination:			Trip Length:
Purpose:		Travel Mode:	
Departure Point:		Arrival Point:	
Stopovers/Connections:			
Documents req'd:			
Carrier (1):	(2):	(3):	
Terminal/Gate Numbers:			
Tickets (if req'd):			
Travel party Names:			
Shuttle/Taxi arrangements:			
Clothing/Personal Items:			
Medicines/Medical:			
Electronics to take:			
Language/translation aids:			
Travel Insurance:			
Pet(s) arrangements:			
Mail/Package pick-up:			
Landscape maintenance arrangement:			
Home security arrangement:			
Food/snacks:			
Bill payment arrangements:			
Other items not covered:			

Link to Page __________

Trip Itinerary

Places to Go:	Notes:

Things to See:	Notes:

Trip Conclusion

Places of Interest		
Date	Location	Category

People Met or Contacts Made		
Date	Name	Addr/Number

Trip Expense Record		
Date	**Description**	**Amount**

Trip Preparation Checklist

Trip:		Start Date:	End Date:
Destination:			Trip Length:
Purpose:		Travel Mode:	
Departure Point:		Arrival Point:	
Stopovers/Connections:			
Documents req'd:			
Carrier (1):	(2):	(3):	
Terminal/Gate Numbers:			
Tickets (if req'd):			

Travel party Names:

Shuttle/Taxi arrangements:

Clothing/Personal Items:

Medicines/Medical:

Electronics to take:

Language/translation aids:

Travel Insurance:

Pet(s) arrangements:

Mail/Package pick-up:

Landscape maintenance arrangement:

Home security arrangement:

Food/snacks:

Bill payment arrangements:

Other items not covered:

Link to Page __________

Trip Itinerary

Places to Go:	Notes:

Things to See:	Notes:

Trip Conclusion

Places of Interest		
Date	Location	Category

People Met or Contacts Made		
Date	Name	Addr/Number

Trip Expense Record		
Date	Description	Amount

Trip Preparation Checklist

Trip:		Start Date:	End Date:
Destination:			Trip Length:
Purpose:		Travel Mode:	
Departure Point:		Arrival Point:	
Stopovers/Connections:			
Documents req'd:			
Carrier (1):	(2):	(3):	
Terminal/Gate Numbers:			
Tickets (if req'd):			
Travel party Names:			
Shuttle/Taxi arrangements:			
Clothing/Personal Items:			
Medicines/Medical:			
Electronics to take:			
Language/translation aids:			
Travel Insurance:			
Pet(s) arrangements:			
Mail/Package pick-up:			
Landscape maintenance arrangement:			
Home security arrangement:			
Food/snacks:			
Bill payment arrangements:			
Other items not covered:			

Link to Page __________

Trip Itinerary

Places to Go:	Notes:

Things to See:	Notes:

Trip Conclusion

Places of Interest		
Date	Location	Category

People Met or Contacts Made		
Date	Name	Addr/Number

Trip Expense Record		
Date	**Description**	**Amount**

Trip Preparation Checklist

Trip:		Start Date:	End Date:
Destination:			Trip Length:
Purpose:		Travel Mode:	
Departure Point:		Arrival Point:	
Stopovers/Connections:			
Documents req'd:			
Carrier (1):	(2):	(3):	
Terminal/Gate Numbers:			
Tickets (if req'd):			
Travel party Names:			
Shuttle/Taxi arrangements:			
Clothing/Personal Items:			
Medicines/Medical:			
Electronics to take:			
Language/translation aids:			
Travel Insurance:			
Pet(s) arrangements:			
Mail/Package pick-up:			
Landscape maintenance arrangement:			
Home security arrangement:			
Food/snacks:			
Bill payment arrangements:			
Other items not covered:			

Link to Page __________

Trip Itinerary

Places to Go:	Notes:

Things to See:	Notes:

Trip Conclusion

Date	Location	Category

People Met or Contacts Made

Date	Name	Addr/Number

Trip Expense Record		
Date	Description	Amount

Trip Preparation Checklist

Trip:	Start Date:	End Date:
Destination:		Trip Length:
Purpose:	Travel Mode:	
Departure Point:	Arrival Point:	

Stopovers/Connections:
Documents req'd:

Carrier (1):	(2):	(3):

Terminal/Gate Numbers:
Tickets (if req'd):
Travel party Names:
Shuttle/Taxi arrangements:
Clothing/Personal Items:
Medicines/Medical:
Electronics to take:
Language/translation aids:
Travel Insurance:
Pet(s) arrangements:
Mail/Package pick-up:
Landscape maintenance arrangement:
Home security arrangement:
Food/snacks:
Bill payment arrangements:
Other items not covered:

Link to Page __________

Trip Itinerary

Places to Go:	Notes:

Things to See:	Notes:

Trip Preparation Checklist

Trip:		Start Date:	End Date:
Destination:			Trip Length:
Purpose:		Travel Mode:	
Departure Point:		Arrival Point:	
Stopovers/Connections:			
Documents req'd:			
Carrier (1):	(2):	(3):	
Terminal/Gate Numbers:			
Tickets (if req'd):			
Travel party Names:			
Shuttle/Taxi arrangements:			
Clothing/Personal Items:			
Medicines/Medical:			
Electronics to take:			
Language/translation aids:			
Travel Insurance:			
Pet(s) arrangements:			
Mail/Package pick-up:			
Landscape maintenance arrangement:			
Home security arrangement:			
Food/snacks:			
Bill payment arrangements:			
Other items not covered:			

Link to Page __________

Trip Itinerary

Places to Go:	Notes:

Things to See:	Notes:

Trip Conclusion

Places of Interest

Date	Location	Category

People Met or Contacts Made

Date	Name	Addr/Number

Trip Expense Record		
Date	Description	Amount

Trip Preparation Checklist

Trip:	Start Date:	End Date:
Destination:		Trip Length:
Purpose:	Travel Mode:	
Departure Point:	Arrival Point:	

Stopovers/Connections:

Documents req'd:

Carrier (1):   (2):   (3):

Terminal/Gate Numbers:

Tickets (if req'd):

Travel party Names:

Shuttle/Taxi arrangements:

Clothing/Personal Items:

Medicines/Medical:

Electronics to take:

Language/translation aids:

Travel Insurance:

Pet(s) arrangements:

Mail/Package pick-up:

Landscape maintenance arrangement:

Home security arrangement:

Food/snacks:

Bill payment arrangements:

Other items not covered:

Link to Page __________

Trip Itinerary

Places to Go:	Notes:

Things to See:	Notes:

Trip Conclusion

Places of Interest		
Date	Location	Category

People Met or Contacts Made		
Date	Name	Addr/Number

Trip Expense Record		
Date	Description	Amount

Trip Preparation Checklist

Trip:		Start Date:	End Date:
Destination:			Trip Length:
Purpose:		Travel Mode:	
Departure Point:		Arrival Point:	
Stopovers/Connections:			
Documents req'd:			
Carrier (1):	(2):	(3):	
Terminal/Gate Numbers:			
Tickets (if req'd):			

Travel party Names:

Shuttle/Taxi arrangements:

Clothing/Personal Items:

Medicines/Medical:

Electronics to take:

Language/translation aids:

Travel Insurance:

Pet(s) arrangements:

Mail/Package pick-up:

Landscape maintenance arrangement:

Home security arrangement:

Food/snacks:

Bill payment arrangements:

Other items not covered:

Link to Page __________

Trip Itinerary

Places to Go:	Notes:

Things to See:	Notes:

Trip Conclusion

Places of Interest		
Date	Location	Category

People Met or Contacts Made		
Date	Name	Addr/Number

Trip Expense Record		
Date	Description	Amount

Section 5 – Entertainment

This section provides some fun activities to make use of travel time that would be wasted watching bad in-flight movies or reading dog-eared airline magazines!

"Games lubricate the body and the mind."
Benjamin Franklin

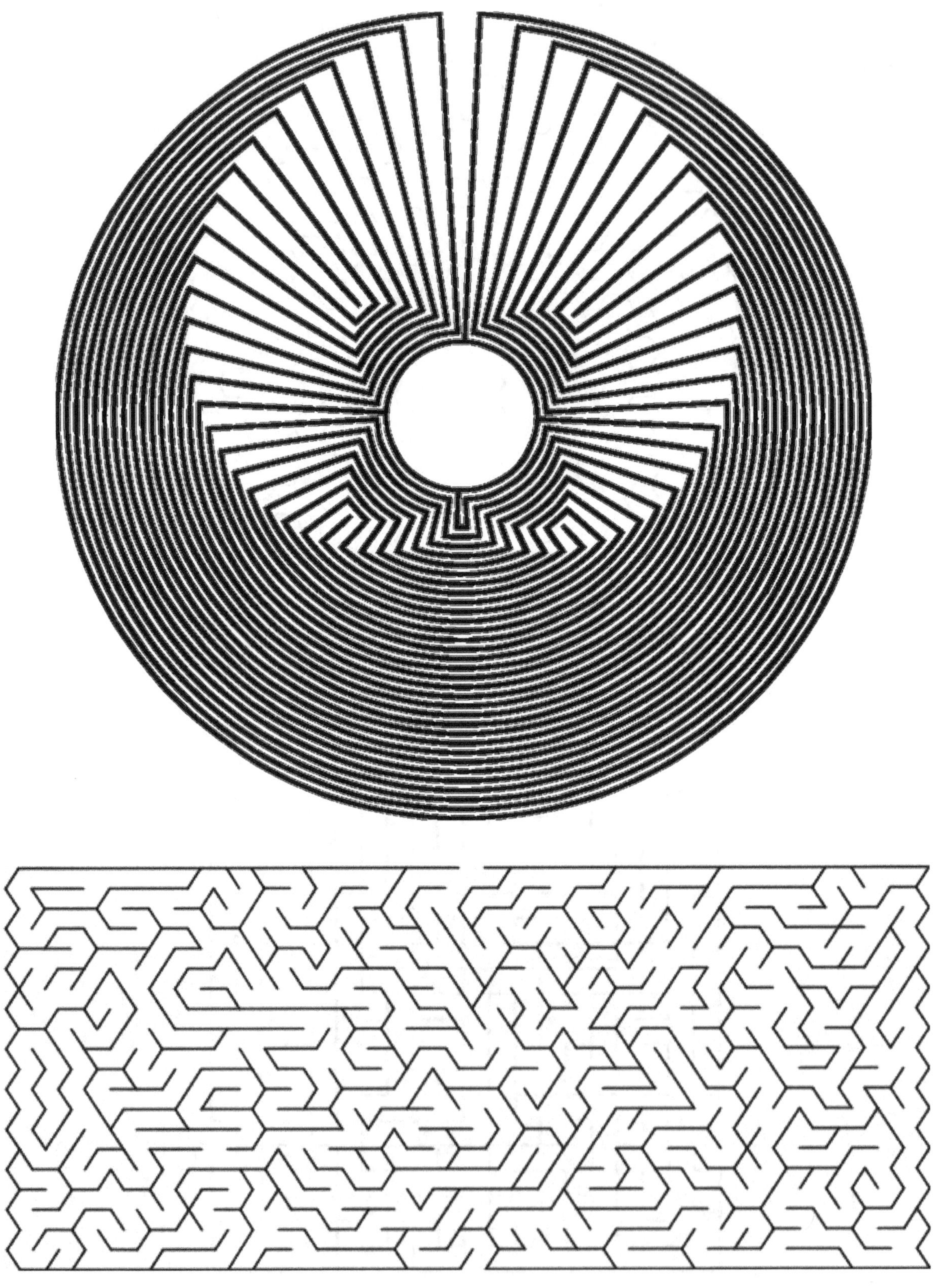

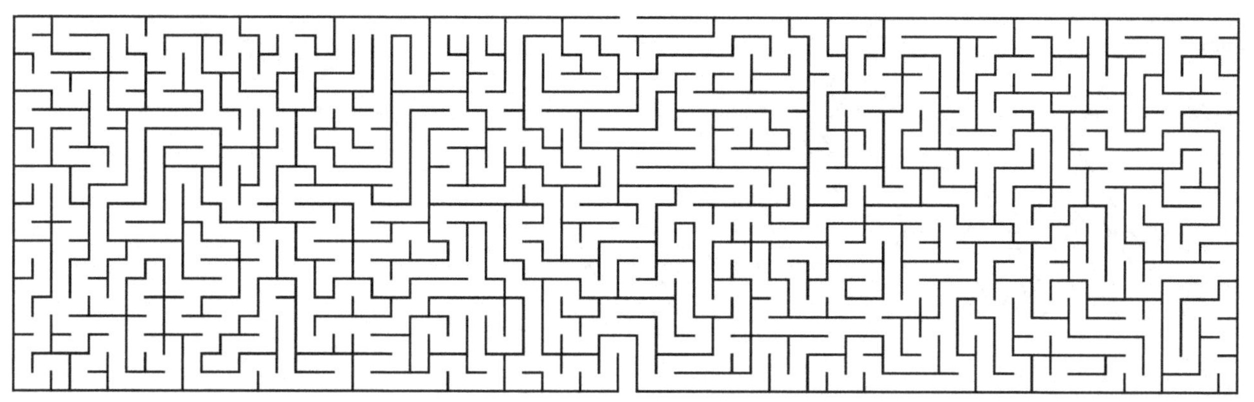

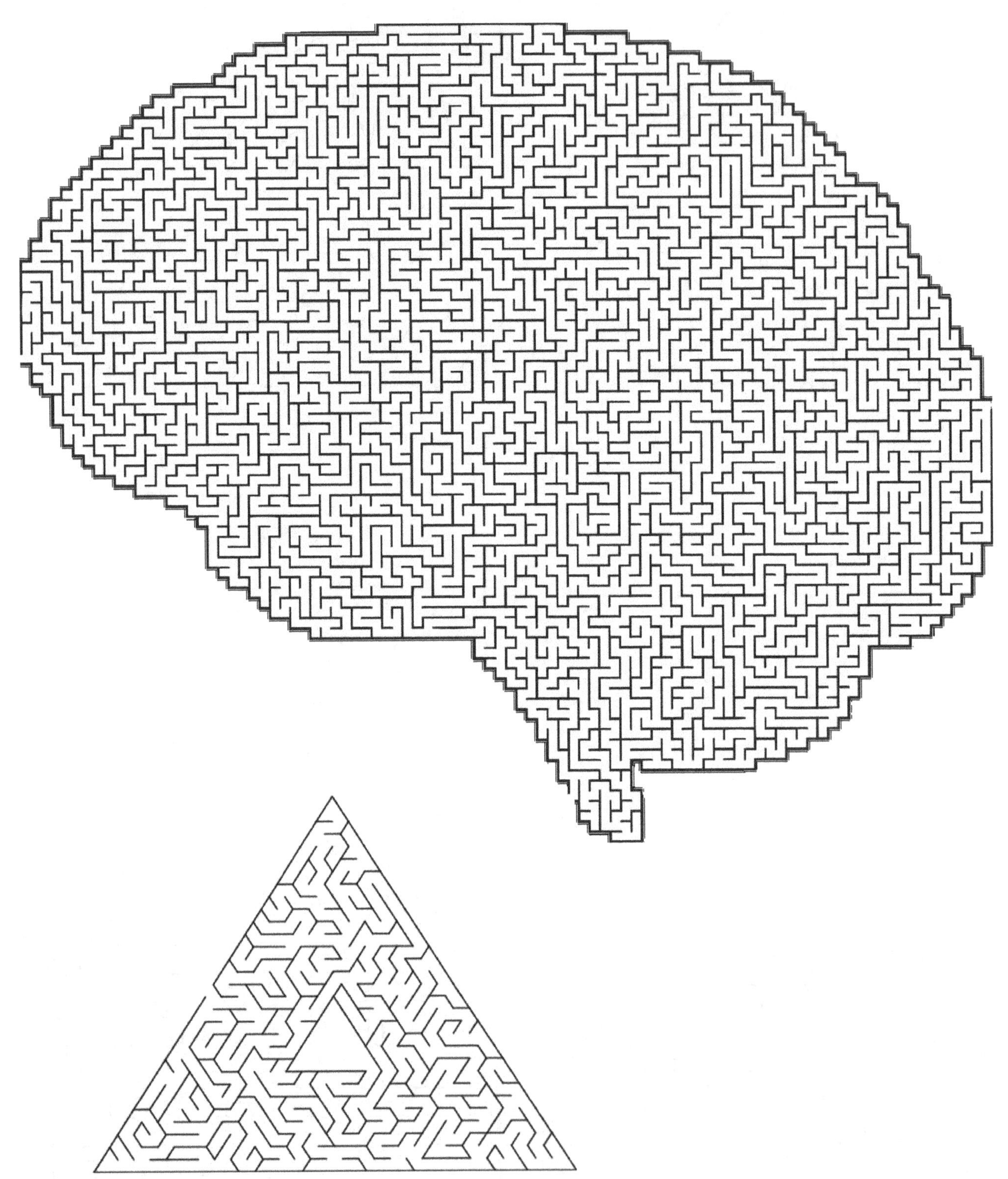

Gadget Book - Air Travel

```
A  L  S  U  Z  H  N  H  V  U  A  I  R  P  O  R  T  H  Q  J  T  J  E
V  Q  S  G  N  I  W  A  W  W  R  E  H  V  O  C  T  U  A  Z  L  F  A
G  Y  S  G  C  S  L  K  V  R  A  M  C  W  M  F  O  H  L  W  A  J  L
M  A  K  Z  Y  N  F  E  Z  I  T  T  G  X  S  J  L  W  M  H  J  M  K
P  W  Q  S  W  V  C  V  Y  U  G  N  B  M  L  W  I  F  F  P  J  J  Y
H  N  T  T  E  R  A  D  I  O  C  A  M  A  I  K  P  R  V  L  E  X  A
Y  U  I  U  W  A  A  V  J  U  G  D  T  X  G  R  O  H  I  F  T  T  I
F  R  P  R  J  R  T  S  A  J  P  N  X  I  S  G  C  S  V  G  W  O  R
U  E  K  B  M  A  G  B  N  G  E  E  N  H  O  O  A  C  D  A  W  W  P
C  B  C  U  B  D  S  Z  E  M  X  T  Z  A  C  N  I  G  K  S  T  E  L
E  K  O  L  H  A  B  I  M  L  X  T  L  E  I  R  N  W  E  D  W  R  A
J  Q  C  E  D  R  L  L  E  A  T  A  Y  I  Y  A  W  K  L  A  W  U  N
G  V  A  N  N  U  Y  E  J  Z  I  G  Q  B  X  M  E  B  A  W  Y  L  E
T  D  O  C  E  F  T  A  R  M  A  C  N  S  P  P  U  E  L  G  E  C  H
T  Q  O  E  T  E  P  P  M  C  C  O  H  F  T  R  A  Y  F  C  N  E  S
U  N  R  A  R  L  C  P  I  L  O  T  V  A  Q  S  G  E  O  J  L  V  G
```

Find the following words in the puzzle.
Words are hidden ↑ ↓ → ← and ↘ .

AIRPLANE	NAVIGATION	TARMAC
AIRPORT	PILOT	TOWER
ATTENDANT	RADAR	TRAY
BAGGAGE	RADIO	TURBULENCE
COCKPIT	RAMP	WALKWAY
COPILOT	RUNWAY	WINGS
JET	SEATBELT	

D S V W Q P O R T Z R E R X S P I H S Y K S N
L F L H T L D O C K J B N K N A C R D V W B K
Q E Q R R B H O Z T U C R K E S I U R C A R T
O U Q D R R U M P F G T E D Z T R M T D N C F
R D V F O I W X M A Q Q T L Q L I R W O B W C
B Y L L H D P C E X O L S R M S Q Z I K I L A
E A P P C G Y I S T A T E R O O M T K M T L P
M L L H N E G A E Q Z L T N Q K M E G S I P T
D G L L A M M S G R Y T H V I H Q Q R T B R A
S E A G A J E K Q B D R A W R O F T H E T S I
I W M N K S Y C D L D R A O B R A T S W V G N
M A U R G I T I A I T A J E S J D L V A L U A
I L P G P W D O I B Z R E D N E T D D R T Q K
D Q W F H L A G S S I D Q T Y E N H T D F M K
Z C F U V O A Y Q Q T N B Y Q S Y M J R G I Y
Y H T R E B M V W D L R C K L P M W T P U A P

Find the following words in the puzzle.
Words are hidden ↑ ↓ → ← and ↘ .

AFT	CAPTAIN	SHIP
ANCHOR	CRUISE	STARBOARD
BALLAST	DOCK	STATEROOM
BERTH	FORWARD	STERN
BOW	GANGWAY	STEWARD
BRIDGE	PIER	TENDER
CABIN	PORT	

```
X D X B U H S R O R R I M A I Z Q A O N C T E
U H H H N E U K F Q W X B R A D A E N X D Y A
G N O V P T N D X P H B H H L O K X Y L Z R W
E Z H O T A W L B E O U Y Y U I S Y G Z Q A D
C Q G Y R T T E A N D A O R L L O T A U P D S
I X F C U S I I Q O U L S T T O L L S I J A A
L W Y X N R R H J I A U V Q Q T M V O S W R U
O Y A B K E E S G T L G Y Y I B B H L S U W T
P M W P Y T T D B C K G N I E E A T I I X V O
U N H Z A N R N H E L A O W F U T B N F A L B
G X G M W I U I X S W G U F L A T W E G H E A
B G I W E Q C W Z R X E J W S P E H S J O Y H
H B H K E J A J L E S V U O P P R A M H O N N
F P J M R C R N E T J C L P Q K Y F Z D D S J
K U W J F O P W S N B H T P R U S A K K M B P
W X G Z L K A E X I W U S P L O G W N U C A Q
```

Find the following words in the puzzle.
Words are hidden ↑ ↓ → ← and ↘ .

AUTOBAHN	HOOD	SUV
BATTERY	INTERSECTION	TIRE
CAR	INTERSTATE	TOLL
FLAT	LUGGAGE	TOLLROAD
FREEWAY	MIRROR	TRUNK
GASOLINE	POLICE	WINDSHIELD
HIGHWAY	RADAR	

```
O M E D I C I N E K K R V R Q P L M M P J C F
W O S S Y Z L X H J P U S S T Q C A H P L P C
Q L U N D D L G O E M Q A T O N O H U R L B R
Y P S I J S V S K X A D I N I M C N W K F U F
D H N A D N C K L Z C K R G L O S P V I S S Y
E T H T C O A O S F U C P I E N M R P J Y E Z
S M A N W I U H A G A A O Q T J A D E R D V A
I F S U P T T G I S J P R C R W R R O Q G I S
U L E O X A O K L H T P T T I H N Q O C Y R B
R O V M I C V A D N E C P V E U I Y E B K D D
C K I H G A M K N I N J S W S B A Z A C W W B
H Y T W S V O H R X P I R T N P R S O O V Y C
R R A W P J K P Y A D I L O H D T D V I T B S
M A L P L I P G O G H U C Q N F A M I L Y T W
A H E W U X D X G M J O C T K X U Z T L V R M
N G R H A M Y Y L F F H S E H T O L C Z N S T
```

Find the following words in the puzzle.
Words are hidden ↑ ↓ → ← and ↘ .

AIRPORT	DOCK	PACK
AUTO	DRIVE	RELATIVES
BUS	FAMILY	TOILETRIES
CAMP	FLY	TRAIN
CLOTHES	HOLIDAY	TRIP
COAST	MEDICINE	VACATION
CRUISE	MOUNTAINS	

Puzzle 1

	6	9				5	2	
7		3		6			1	
1		4	9		5	7	6	3
	4	1	8		3			
9	8			1		4		7
3	7	6			4	2		1
4		8					7	2
5		7		2	9		4	8
	3	2		4	8	1	9	5

Puzzle 2

2	9	7		6	4	1		5
		3			1	2		8
5		1	2		7			
		9		5		4		
8			3	4	6		9	7
	5		7			3	1	
1		8	6			9	5	
	4		9	5		7		1
9	7			1	2	6		

Puzzle 3

			9	7	4		8	1
7	9	3		1			5	
			5		3	6		7
2		9			7	8		6
3							7	5
			6	3	5	4		
8				9	1	5		
6				5	8			3
		5		6	2	7	4	

Puzzle 4

	5			7	9			
6		1				9	4	
			6					
9	3		5	2		4		7
7		4	3			2		5
2	1	5			4	3	8	
4	2	3					7	
	6					5		
		8	1		7		2	4

Puzzle 5

1		8			4		9	
	7			9	8	2		
9		4	3	6				8
				8	9	4		
2		7	4	1	5	6		
			6	2	3			1
8	4			3		5		
	6					7		3
7	3	9	8		6			2

Puzzle 6

	9		8	5			6	
2		6		3	9			
	5		2				9	
	6	2	7		1	4	5	9
5				2		7	8	
8		9			6			1
7	3	8	6	1	2	9		5
9		4		7	5	6		8
	1			9			2	7

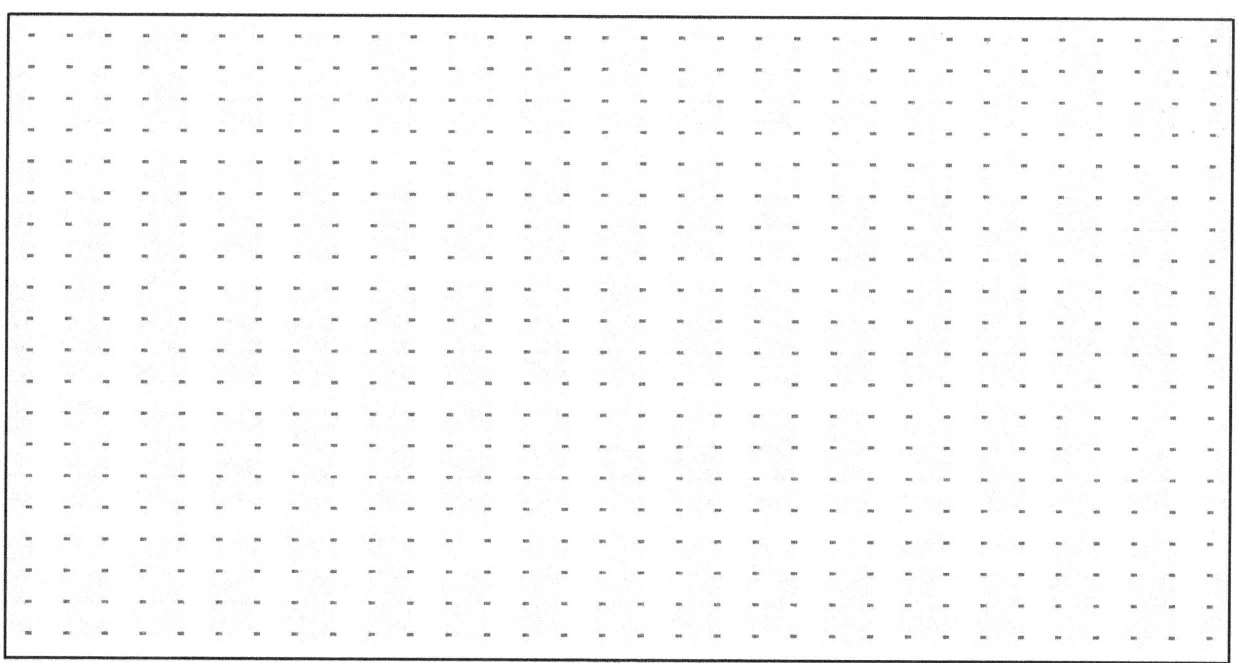

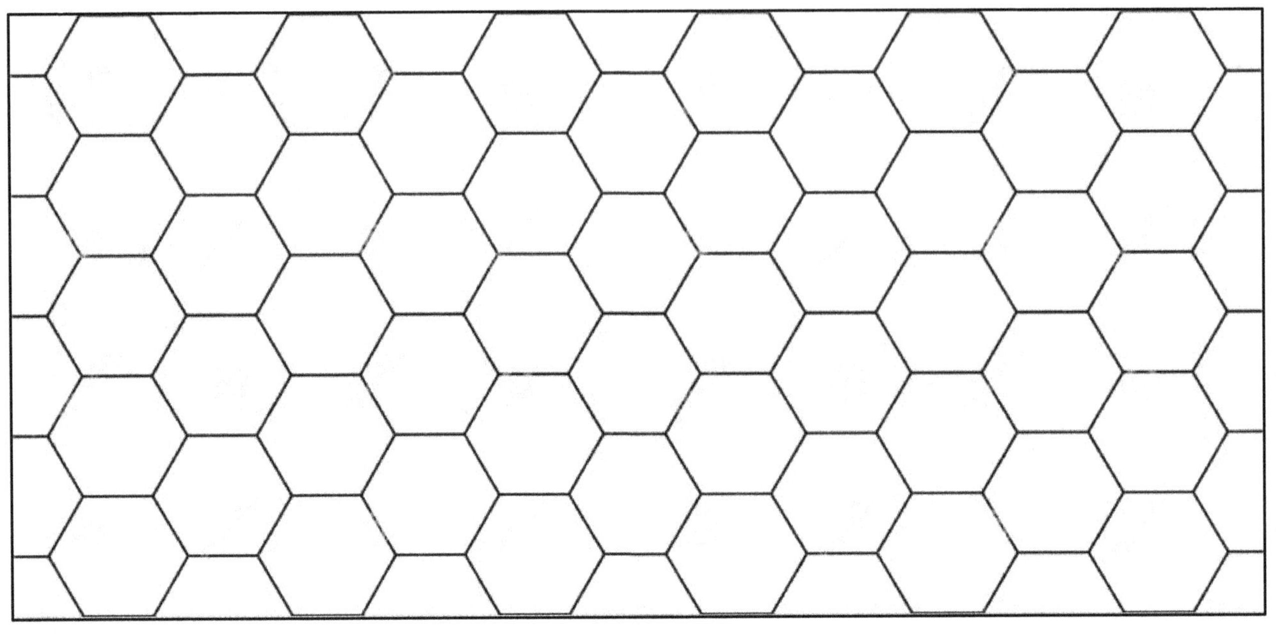

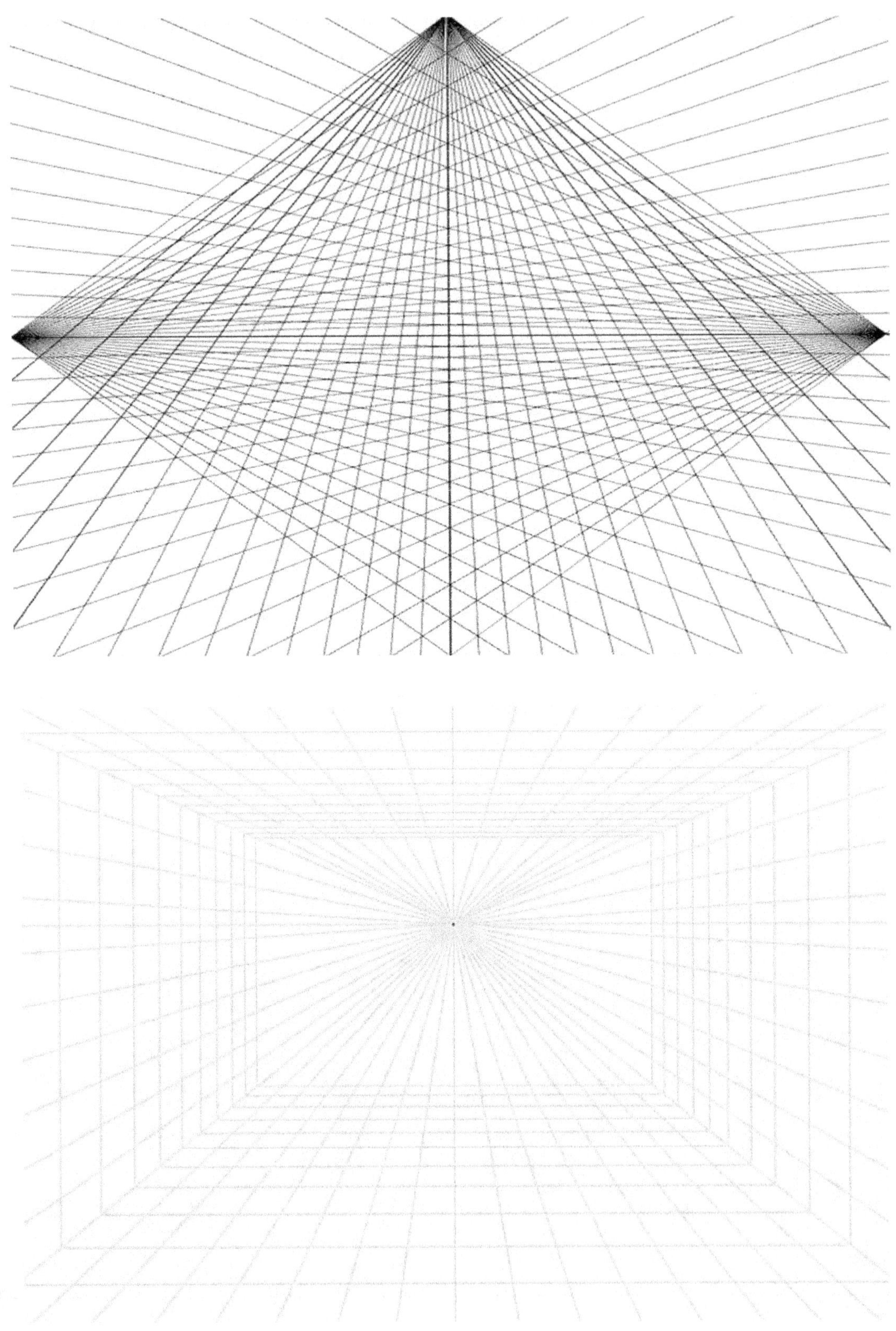

Music
Composition?

[145]

CONCLUSION

I Hope you enjoyed using this journal and with it, helped organize your travel activities.

If you like this book format, please leave an honest review on Amazon or other sources.

J. Ronald Adair

Email: jradair@eltekpublishing.com Website: www.eltekpublishing.com

In addition to the 'Gadget Book' series, here are other works found on Amazon by the Author/Publisher:

	"Killer" 42 (a how-to book on playing the domino game '42' at a high level) Sold on Amazon as both a paperback and Kindle book. Website: www.killer42.com
	Grandparents and parents! Save your Millennial family members. You know they are clueless in many ways. This book is THE book to help them navigate through the complexities of life! If you are a Millennial or a Gen Z'er, and wonder why you seem to be always in trouble with just daily problems, then you MUST have this book! www.clueless101.com
	Stressed out? Had enough of the demanding modern world and would like to jump off the runaway 'progress' train? This book shows you how! By applying the points presented, you too can gain control of your finances, time, family functionality, and peace of mind. This book is a humorous look at human nature, 'progress', and the many ways today's Luddite rebels are still flailing away! www.embracingluddism.com